AF255264

Be Still And Know

Copyright © 2019 by James R. Reish
All rights reserved. In accordance with the U.S. Copyright Act of 1976, no part of this book may be reproduced, distributed, or transmitted in any form or by any means, or stored in a database or retrieval system, without the prior written permission of the publisher.

Unless otherwise indicated, all scripture taken from the King James Version of the Bible.

ISBN: 9781096442431

Be Still And Know

Fresh Insights From Psalm 46:10

Jim Reish

Dedication

I dedicate this book to my Lord and Savior, Jesus Christ. Thank you for saving me and giving me a love for Your Word.

And I also dedicate this to my loving wife, Janean, for her ongoing love, help and support.

Contents

Introduction   **9**

Chapter 1:

Be   **11**

Chapter 2:

Be Still   **17**

Chapter 3:

Be Still And Know   **25**

Chapter 4:

Be Still And Know That I Am God   **35**

Introduction

Many people are familiar with **Psalm 46:10**, which instructs us to be still and know that the Lord is God. This book examines that verse and breaks down what it means related to our identity in Christ. We will explore what it means to know God and how knowing Him will show us who He has destined for us to be. We can be as close to God as we decide to be. As we make the choice to draw near to Him, He will draw near to us, and we will experience the satisfaction that only He can give. When we take time to be with Jesus, He will fill us up with Himself, allowing us to know Him in a deeper way.

So, pull up a chair, press the pause button, and be still and know that He is God. The presence of the Lord can do more for us in a moment than anyone else could do for us in a lifetime.

Dr. Jim Reish

Chapter 1

Be

Psalms 46:10 says *"Be still, and know that I am God."* In this chapter, we will discover some amazing things that will help us to know God and be who God made us to be.

First, to know ourselves, we must know God, for He created us and knows us. Therefore, it makes sense to let Him show us who He made us to be.

The initial step is to be born again by accepting Jesus as your Lord and Savior. If you are not born again, simply pray this prayer out loud and from the heart:

God, I believe Jesus is the Son of God. I believe He died for me and my sins on the cross. I believe that You raised Him from the dead on the third day. Jesus, forgive me of my sins and come into my heart. With my heart, I believe You are the Son of God, and

*with my mouth I confess You as Lord. According to
Romans 10:10, I am now saved and born again.
I am God's very own child. I turn from sin and allow
You to live Your life through me for the rest of my
life. In the name of Jesus I pray.*

For those who are born again, it is important to learn
who God made you to be. **II Corinthians 5:17** says
*"Therefore if any man be in Christ, he is a new
creature: old things are passed away; behold, all
things are become new."* You are a new creature in
Christ. That means you have a brand new spirit. **II
Corinthians 5:21** says that you have a right spirit.
You are right with God. You are His very own child,
and you have a right to be who God made you to be.

The way we start to be who God made us to be is by
doing what **Romans 12:2** commands us to do.

> *And be not conformed to this world: but be ye
> transformed by the renewing of your mind, that
> ye may prove what is that good, and*

As we read God's Word, we begin to get God's thoughts, and we begin to think like Him. For example, when someone is rude to us, the Bible tells us to love others, even enemies. So, we purposely choose to think thoughts of love, and we say things like, "I love that person." We may not feel like it in our emotions, but we can choose God's way rather than the way of our feelings. By thinking right and speaking right we are empowered to act right, which brings right results.

We must agree with God by saying what God says about us. When we sin we do not have to be condemned, but we can confess our sins to the Lord and He will forgive us and cleanse us. Because we are the righteousness of God in Christ we have a right to get right with God whenever we mess up. Then we can continue living right with His help.

As we renew our minds, speak God's Word, and do the Word, we will be who God says we are. Say who

God says you are, and you become it. For example, your circumstances may say that you're broke, but God says you are blessed. Who you believe and agree with will determine the outcome. The words we speak, especially if they agree with God, have transforming power.

When we are born again, everything God says we are is in seed form inside us. So, now we need to water the seed to grow into who He made us to be. Your body may say you are sick, but the Word declares you are healed. Declaring God's Word about our health and acting like it is a done deal will cause the seed of faith to grow and healing to manifest in our physical bodies. We must act like we are healed before we see it. We do this by doing something we could not do before. As we take a step of faith, God will meet us where we are. The step of faith releases God to do what only He can, bringing healing to our bodies. Then we have become outwardly what we already were inwardly! You see, **I Peter 2:24** says we **were** already healed. And if we **were** healed, then we **are** healed- and acting in faith makes it a reality. Therefore, we can be healed, because the seed of the Word says we are healed. We can walk in blessing because the Word says we're already are blessed. When we walk in the promises of the Word and act as if they are so, the seed of the Word grows in us to full maturity and we experience the results.

Who we are on the inside has to get on the outside to do us any good. It's like a farmer who has a bag of seeds but refuses to plant them. Unless he sows those seeds and tends them, he will not experience a harvest. Plant the Word in you and reap the benefits.

It has been said that God called us human beings, not human doings. We are not robots, but we are created by God with a free will. We need to choose to be at peace in being who God made us, and not trying to work to become something. Just relax and be. When we decide to be the new creation, the children of God He made us to be, then we will produce what we want in our lives out of who we already are in Him. We must be at peace with who He has made us to be. We must accept ourselves. Just be the best you that you can be. There's no one else like you, and no one else can take your place.

Always remember the process. We are becoming on the outside who God already made us on the inside. We are victorious, blessed, loved, forgiven, and accepted. When we know who God is in us and who we are in Christ, God will help us walk out what He put in us. We are free to be ourselves without comparing and competing with each other. Why? Because all we are aiming at is being the best version of ourselves possible, following Jesus as our perfect example.

In summary, renew your mind to the Word of God, for only He can show you the real you. Speak His Word. God spoke what He wanted to see, saying "Light, be," and light was. Speak who He says you are and you will become it. Act on God's Word because it has the power to make you what God made you to be. And walk in the freedom of knowing you can be yourself. Say it out loud, "I'm free to be me, in Jesus' Name."

Chapter 2

Be Still

We continue our examination of **Psalms 46:10**, which says, *"Be still, and know that I am God."* The phrase "be still" in the Hebrew can be translated "let go." We need to let go of the things that are preventing God from being God in our lives.

Letting go is a hard and costly lesson to learn- trust me, I know. We can save ourselves a lot of heartache, time, and trouble by learning to let go. The quicker we let go and allow the Lord to have control, the sooner He can go to work on our behalf. It is not worth it to hold onto things or people or situations when they are not God's best for us. We need to let go of whatever we have allowed to take priority over God in our lives. As we do, God will become our central focus; our first love.

We're letting go of this world so we can give God His proper place. We can then exalt God and put Him on the throne of our hearts and lives. Then we will see

Him do what we could not have done ourselves.

Be still and let go. It is a key to victory. When your enemy comes against you, be still and let go. I like what Moses told the children of Israel when the Egyptian army pursued them to the Red Sea. The Israelites were trapped, unable to go forward or backward. What do you do when you face a situation like this?

> *And Moses said unto the people, Fear ye not, stand still, and see the salvation of the LORD, which he will shew to you to day: for the Egyptians whom ye have seen to day, ye shall see them again no more for ever.*
>
> *The LORD shall fight for you, and ye shall hold your peace.* **Exodus 14:13-14 (KJV)**

It is time to be still and let the Lord fight your fight. Let go of control. Stand still; and hold onto your peace as God fights for you and wins. It is time to be quiet about the situation. It's time to start trusting and not striving or worrying. Don't try to defeat the enemy yourself. The battle is not yours; it is the Lord's.

Peace is a place of power. It can silence your critics. It can stop strife right in its tracks. You never have to defend yourself or defend God because the battle belongs to the Lord. Peace is a place of power and protection. In **Exodus 14**, God told Moses to stretch out his rod. When he did, the Red Sea parted and they were able to walk through on dry ground, delivering them from the Egyptians. The rod represents God's Word. When we lift up God's Word and stretch it out over our circumstances, He delivers us. In the same way that Moses stretched forth the rod, we speak forth the Word of God to release our faith.

When we lose our peace, we don't think, act, or speak correctly, and we try to take care of things on our own, which does not work. Being still and keeping our peace removes us from responsibility and places the responsibility for the battle in God's hands. He will do a better job than we could ever do. When we stress, we miss God's best. And God's best is victory; all the time, every time.

And Moses stretched forth his hand over the

sea, and the sea returned to his strength when the morning appeared; and the Egyptians fled against it; and the LORD overthrew the Egyptians in the midst of the sea. **Exodus 14:27 (KJV)**

God drowned Pharaoh and his army in the Red Sea. Give your situation to God, hold your peace, and watch Him fight your battle- and your enemy you will see no more. Israel never had to deal with the army of Egypt ever again.

Egypt represents the world's bondage. When we trust God, He will liberate us from every bondage that is in the world. Whether it is sickness, failure, hurt, debt- whatever- He has drowned it in the sea, never to rise again.

When something comes against us, it is not time to panic or fear. We cannot hear God in that frame of mind. You must know who you are in Christ. You must be who you are on the inside in order to overcome what is coming against you on the outside.

Remind yourself that greater is He that is in you than he that is in the world. As you are still before God, you can hear God and get His direction. This will allow you to take the right step to walk in victory over the enemy. Feeding on and acting on God's Word will make us stronger on the inside so we can overcome what is on the outside.

When you have done your best and it seems that it's not enough, cast your care on the Lord. Just rest, letting God work it out. Remember- when we rest, God works; but when we work, God rests. When we believe God's Word and trust in His power, we rest.

> *For we which have believed do enter into rest, as he said, As I have sworn in my wrath, if they shall enter into my rest: although the works were finished from the foundation of the world.*
> **Hebrews 4:3 (KJV)**

If you're not resting, you're not believing. I like what **Psalm 37:7** says: *Rest in the LORD, and wait patiently for him.* Resting is part of being still. God wants us full of peace, trusting and resting in Him. We must remember the finished work of Christ. When He said, "It is finished," He was saying, "Paid in full." This means we rest from a position of completed victory, not trying to fight the fight, but trusting in what Jesus has already done. It is not about what we can do for God, but what He has already done for us. As we get still before God, we can position ourselves to receive all that He has already provided.

> *Blessed be the God and Father of our Lord Jesus Christ, who hath blessed us with all spiritual blessings in heavenly places in Christ.* ***Ephesians 1:3 (KJV)***

> *According as his divine power hath given unto us all things that pertain unto life and godliness, through the knowledge of him that hath called us to glory and virtue.* ***II Peter 1:3 (KJV)***

God has already blessed us and given us all things that pertain to life and godliness. All we need to do is believe. Believing positions us to receive from God what already belongs to us. Be still, and receive everything God has for you in Christ.

Chapter 3

Be Still And Know

We are furthering our analysis of **Psalm 46:10**. We now add to what we have studied and we are discussing "Be still and know." As we expand our understanding of this verse, we now look at getting knowledge of God's will and direction.

In becoming who God made us to be, we learn to be still for we have found a place of rest. We find our identity in who God is and who we are in Christ. As long as we fail to see who we are in Christ, there will always be a seeking, a searching for who we are. However, as we follow the direction to "be still and know," we will know who God made us to be, and then we will know what He wants us to do. Remember, our "doing" should always come out of our "being;" who God made us to be in Christ. And if we're not still, if we don't let go and rest, then we will not know God's will.

Knowing comes from slowing down long enough to **listen**, **learn**, and then **live**. When we need answers, we need to seek God by seeking His Word. God and His Word are the same.

> *In the beginning was the Word, and the Word was with God, and the Word was God.* ***John 1:1 (KJV)***

Before we make any decisions, especially major decisions like where to live, what church to attend, who to marry, and so on, we need to be still and know by seeking God in His Word.

> *But stand thou still a while, that I may shew thee the word of God.* ***I Samuel 9:27b (KJV)***

As we seek God and His Word, we may not know every single step that our journey requires. However, when we take a step, God's Word will illuminate just enough of our path so we can see to take the next step. Here's a recent example from my own life:

My wife and I were seeking the Lord about going to

church in Texas. The issue was that we lived in South Carolina. We needed to see if God would open a door for us to move to Texas. First, we visited Texas and did some research about the area in Texas we were considering. Then, we put our home in South Carolina up for sale. We then flew to Texas for a follow-up visit and to look at places to live. On that trip, we found an apartment that met all our needs and was just a few miles from the church; it had just opened up. Although we had no income source at the time, we were given favor and our lease application was accepted. After finding the apartment, we accepted an offer on our home. We moved and God has met every need we have had since. I wanted a place to take walks, and we found a park just a couple miles away. I wanted to be able to go to a good chiropractor, and there is one just up the road. As we kept taking steps, we were able to get direction on the next step to take. We were seeking God all along the way.

The Bible says in **Psalm 37:23** that God orders, establishes, and guides our steps. However, we must always put His Word first.

> *But seek ye first the kingdom of God, and his righteousness; and all these things shall be added unto you.* **Matthew 6:33 (KJV)**

When we seek God first and His kingdom, the other things we want and need will fall in line. We are to seek God, not things. When we do, we will mature and God can give us things, since we will be able to handle them. This usually means that we are to sit a while and seek Him. The more we seek God and obey His direction, the wiser we become and the better our lives will be.

Bear in mind, there are some things we will not know or learn any other way except by sitting still in His presence, listening and learning. As we go through life, we can learn things the hard way or the right way. The hard way is to not allow the Lord to direct our paths, or to fail to do what we hear the Lord tell us. For example, **Luke 6:38** says we are to give in order to receive. However, we can choose to be selfish and just take, take, take without giving. We will find this leads to an unfulfilling and empty life, plus it is a good way to lose loved ones and friends. On the other hand, we can learn the right way by listening to God and doing what His Word says: "Give and it shall be given."

Their strength is to sit still. **Isaiah 30:7b (KJV)**

Isn't that a thought-provoking statement? Our strength is found in inactivity? Yes, it can be. For example, when someone comes against us, we don't need to take matters into our own hands to get revenge or even to clear our own name. When we sit still and give it to God to handle, it always turns out better. Plus, we won't get ourselves stressed out in the process. The devil will try to wear out the saints by trying to engage us in fights and battles that God never called us to fight.

For thus saith the Lord GOD, the Holy One of Israel; In returning and rest shall ye be saved; in quietness and in confidence shall be your strength: and ye would not. **Isaiah 30:15 (KJV)**

The next time trouble comes, be still and know. In other words, get quiet before the Lord and ask Him what He wants you to do. You may just hear Him say, "Do nothing," for as we turn to God, we find rest in Him and we are saved. Saved from what? Any trouble that is coming against us. It goes on to tell us that in quietness and confidence we get our strength. The last four words are interesting: "and ye would not." Wow, God is offering to us, just as He did to the Israelites, an answer to what we face. They did not take it. Why? They refused to return to God to get His help because, like most people, they thought they could solve their own problems. Whether it was pride, selfishness, the flesh, immaturity, or whatever, they chose to take the more difficult way instead of God's way.

When we don't learn our lessons, we are subject to repeat them and to go through the same tests over and over again. We end up in the same pattern, going through the same testing until we learn our lesson and learn it well. When we get still, listen to God, receive His direction, and obey it, the lessons are easier to learn and progress comes faster. Sadly, some people never learn from their mistakes, but lay the blame on others. They are doomed to repeat the same lessons over and over, all the while refusing to accept responsibility. The next time you are tempted to blame someone else for your problems, just be still, know what God is saying to you, and use it to learn, pass the test, and move on.

When we take time to be still, we get to know more about God, ourselves, and other people. We gain insight on things like our finances, how we are treating others, how well we are stewarding what we have been given, and whether we are in faith about who God intends us to be and what He wants us to do. We can learn so much about life, people, and so on, but many of us are never still long enough to know what God is saying. The more effort we give to being still before the Lord, the more we will know what He is saying.

We will get a deeper connection with our own hearts and more clearly understand our desires, hopes, and dreams, and how they align with the plan of God. Being still is beneficial for many reasons. The more we are still, the more we will know, because we always learn more when we listen more.

> *Wherefore, my beloved brethren, let every man be swift to hear, slow to speak, slow to wrath.*
> ***James 1:19 (KJV)***

When we are still, we learn to respond correctly when negative things are happening to us. Because we have been in the presence of God, we will respond in love rather than hate, with patience rather than frustration, and with faith rather than fear. As we are still, we will hold our peace and walk in calm delight, giving glory to God.

Near the beginning of this chapter I mentioned listen, learn, and live. We need to listen to God and His Word, and the people God has placed in authority over us. Doing so enables us to learn. We can learn from nearly anyone if we are meek enough to receive from them. Meekness means that we are teachable and able to receive knowledge, instruction, and correction from others. And learning what God is trying to teach us makes our lives better. As we listen, and learn, we will live the life God has for us.

Incorporating the following practices in our lives will help us in our efforts to **be still and know**.

- Spend regular time studying God's Word. **II Timothy 2:15**

- Spend daily time in prayer. **Ephesians 5:18**

- Pursue only godly relationships. **Proverbs 13:20, Proverbs 18:24, Proverbs 27:17**

- Give. **Luke 6:38, Malachi 3:10-11**

- Witness and share the Lord with others. **Mark 16:15-20, Luke 5:10, Acts 1:8, Acts 4:33**

- Attend church. **Hebrews 10:25**

- Spend time worshipping God. **John 4:23-24**

Chapter 4

Be Still And Know That I Am God

*Be still, and know that I am God: I will be exalted among the heathen, I will be exalted in the earth. **Psalm 46:10 (KJV)***

To know God, we must take time to learn about Him. We must want Him more than anything else. We need to hunger and thirst after God, then seek Him until we're filled- filled with His Word, His Spirit, His presence, and all He is. We put God first and keep Him first in our lives as we seek Him through His Word, prayer, fellowship, worship, and yes, even fasting.

The more we seek God, the more we find Him. The more we find Him, the more we experience His love, His presence, His power, provision, protection, guidance, and so on. Only God can satisfy us- spirit, soul, and body. And we can know Him more and more through spending time in His Word. To thrive in God, our spirits need to be born-again and baptized in the Holy Spirit as detailed in **Acts 2:4** with the evidence of speaking in tongues. Our spirits also need to feed on God's Word daily. God is a personal God and He wants us to know Him through His Word and Spirit.

I have found it very helpful to systematically read and study the Bible, whether going through the entire Word or digging into a specific book, such as Psalms, Proverbs or one of the epistles. I recommend using a good study Bible, along with other reference materials, asking the Holy Spirit to lead you and guide you into all truth. He will use scripture to explain scripture because the Word interprets itself. A word of caution: don't pull a verse or passage out of context. Pulling a text out of context causes the original circumstances surrounding it to be lost, which can cause us to misunderstand scripture's message and can lead to serious error. If you don't understand something you read in the Word, learn to wait for God to explain it to you. He will definitely do so, sometimes right away, sometimes later. He can use many ways to do this such as a book, a friend, or a message you hear preached, to name a few. It is God's will for us to know and understand how to apply scripture to our lives. The important thing is not to make a law out of what we study or how we do it. Instead we should study His Word because we want to, not because we think we have to. God loves us whether we read, study, meditate, confess, sing or pray the scriptures- or not. The reason we study is to know God and His Word. God already knows His Word. He wrote it especially for us so we can know Him. Let's explore some aspects of who God's Word says He is.

God is love.

> *He that loveth not knoweth not God; for God is love.* ***I John 4:8 (KJV)***

God will always love you. Always. Forever. No matter what. Stop for a minute and let that sink in. God loves you now and He always will.

God is good.

When things go badly, God will turn it to good. According to Psalm 119:68, God is good and He does good.

> *And we know that all things work together for good to them that love God, to them who are the called according to his purpose.* **Romans 8:28 (KJV)**

God is just.

God takes wrong things and makes them right, and even better than if it never happened. God will do such a work that you will rejoice in His justice.

> *If we confess our sins, he is faithful and just to forgive us our sins, and to cleanse us from all unrighteousness.* **I John 1:9 (KJV)**

God is faithful.

The Lord is trustworthy, reliable, and dependable. He will do what He says.

I Corinthians 1:9 (KJV)

God keeps His Word. He's always there for us, and He will always come through. He does not change; He is the same yesterday, today, and forever. What God did in the past, He will do today and always.

God is all-knowing.

Theologians call this the omniscience of God. God knows all. He knows you, and He loves you. He knows who you are and where you are. He knows your every desire and need, and He is able to take care of them all.

O Lord, thou hast searched me, and known me. Thou knowest my downsitting and mine uprising, thou understandest my thought afar off. Thou compassest my path and my lying down, and art acquainted with all my ways. For there is not a word in my tongue, but, lo, O LORD, thou knowest it altogether.

Thou hast beset me behind and before, and laid thine hand upon me. Such knowledge is too wonderful for me; it is high, I cannot attain unto it. **Psalm 139:1-6 (KJV)**

God is ever-present.

There is nowhere you can go that God is not there. No person or thing can keep God away. No prison can keep Him out. No pain can stop Him from coming into your heart to save and heal. Wherever you go, He is there, helping you in all you have to do.

Whither shall I go from thy spirit? or whither shall I flee from thy presence? If I ascend up into heaven, thou art there: if I make my bed in hell, behold, thou art there. If I take the wings of the morning, and dwell in the uttermost parts of the sea; Even there shall thy hand lead me, and thy right hand shall hold me. If I say, Surely the darkness shall cover me; even the night shall be light about me. Yea, the darkness hideth not from thee; but the night shineth as the day: the darkness and the light are both alike to thee. For thou hast possessed my reins: thou hast covered me in my mother's womb. I will praise thee; for I am fearfully and wonderfully made: marvellous are thy works; and that my soul knoweth right well. My substance was not hid from thee, when I was made in secret, and curiously wrought in the lowest parts of the earth. Thine eyes did see my substance, yet being unperfect; and in thy book all my members were written, which in continuance were fashioned, when as yet there was none of them. How precious also are thy thoughts unto me, O God! how great is the sum of them! If I should count them, they are more in number than the sand: when I awake, I am still with thee. **Psalm 139:7-18 (KJV)**

God is all-powerful.

He has the power to stop sin, the devil, sickness, lack and anything else. When we give Him access to our lives, He has the power to make a way where there is no way. His power can stop any enemy, and He has given His power to us. As we speak and act on His Word, we will see God go to work, releasing His mighty power on our behalf. The Lord's power breaks bondages and brings blessing.

> *Ah Lord GOD! behold, thou hast made the heaven and the earth by thy great power and stretched out arm, and there is nothing too hard for thee: Thou shewest lovingkindness unto thousands, and recompensest the iniquity of the fathers into the bosom of their children after them: the Great, the Mighty God, the LORD of hosts, is his name.* **Jeremiah 32:17-18 (KJV)**

As we learn God's Word, we will learn God's ways, for they are one and the same. The Lord's ways are ways of love, giving, forgiveness, peace, joy, and righteousness. As we know God's ways, we will understand what God wants us to be and do in life, because He wants us to be like Him. We must slow down and take time to know God by spending time with Him. Maybe you think you don't have a lot of time to spend with God. Then start with what you have.

- Take five minutes to read scripture.
- Take five minutes to pray.
- Take five minutes to sing and worship the Lord.

As you sow this small amount of time to Him, God will multiply your time. You will reap more available time. You will begin to see tasks completed faster and free time open up for you to spend it with Him. That is the harvest you are reaping from sowing a little of your time to be with Him. The bottom line is, we will find time for what we value the most. As we spend time with God, the more time we will find to spend with Him, for we will come to find out that nothing is more important than our time with the Lord in His Word and in His presence.

Draw nigh to God, and he will draw nigh to

We choose how close we want to be with God. As we get close to God, He will reveal and manifest Himself to us in so many ways. We will experience His love, power, provision, and favor, just to name a few.

As we slow down and get to know God, we will learn about Him bit by bit, scripture upon scripture, line upon line, and by His working in our hearts and lives. As we put God first, He will work in such wonderful and amazing ways. As a result, we will know, and so will those around us, that the Lord is God. And that is the manifestation that comes from being still and knowing that He is God.

As I close this book, I'd like to make mention of the name *I Am*. God told Moses in Exodus 3, "I Am that I Am." When Jesus came to the earth, He declared what many call "The Seven I Am's." These are found in the Gospel of John, and they reveal the Lord as the great *I Am*. He is whatever we need Him to be.

1. **I Am the Bread of Life.** Jesus satisfies every hunger. *John 6:35*

2. **I Am the Light of the World.** Follow Jesus and you will never walk in darkness. *John 8:12*

3. **I Am the Door.** Jesus is the open door to knowing God. God can put you in places that no man can. *John 10:7*

4. **I Am the Good Shepherd.** Jesus watches over, feeds, and cares for His own. *John 10:11*

5. **I Am the Resurrection and the Life.** Jesus came to resurrect our dead spirits and give us eternal life. He brings God's life to our spirits, and when a believer dies, he is resurrected to life again. *John 11:25-26*

6. **I Am the Way, the Truth, and the Life.** Jesus is the only way to God. He is the Word of Truth. Jesus came to bring us back into relationship and fellowship with God, giving us eternal life. *John 14:6*

7. **I Am the True Vine.** Jesus is the vine and we are the branches. As we stay attached to Him

and remain in Him, we draw life and bear fruit. When we abide, live, and continue in Christ, He will provide all we need. *John 15:1*

As you continue to pursue the Lord, make the time to be still and truly know that He is God.

> *Be still, and know that I am God: I will be exalted among the heathen, I will be exalted in the earth.* **Psalm 46:10 (KJV)**

www.ingramcontent.com/pod-product-compliance
Lightning Source LLC
Chambersburg PA
CBHW071524030726

47593CB00003B/1381